T0113499

TWENTY-NINE WEEKS
and ONE DAY

MARKETTA SMITH

WESTBOW
PRESS®
A DIVISION OF THOMAS NELSON
& ZONDERVAN

WestBow Press books may be ordered through booksellers or by contacting:

WestBow Press
A Division of Thomas Nelson & Zondervan
1663 Liberty Drive
Bloomington, IN 47403
www.westbowpress.com
1 (866) 928-1240

ISBN: 978-1-9736-0288-0 (sc)
ISBN: 978-1-9736-0287-3 (e)

Library of Congress Control Number: 2017914610

Print information available on the last page.

WestBow Press rev. date: 10/05/2017

In loving memory

of

Naomi Marie Smith,

my

inspiration.

May

you

rest

in

love.

I stepped out on faith because of you. Mommy,

Daddy, and Big Brother love you.

Contents

Introduction

The experience of childbirth is amazing. It's a part of life for some women that defines their whole being. On the other hand, the loss of a child is painful. Faith and strength are needed to get through any unfortunate experience in life. Activating the two is the most difficult thing when enduring such a tragic event.

On February 5, 2017, I became the mother of my second child, Naomi Marie. On that same day, I mourned her death. My journey after loss began the start of my new normal. Life had a new meaning, a new definition, and a new reason. I became solely dependent on Jesus Christ for my complete healing and strength. The plans my husband

and I had for our family were changed forever. We became the parents of an angel.

God does mysterious things for the bettering of his children. He never allows us to go through more than we can handle, even when we have given up. My story is my testimony. It doesn't matter what you have been through with God; you can conquer mountains. Speak life, and remember, with every step you take you are one step closer to your destiny and the promise that God has for your life. We were human, we had feelings, and we mourned the loss of our daughter. In the scripture, Exodus 14:14 reads, "The Lord will fight for you; you need only to be still."

There is a sense of peace in knowing that God fights for his children. When you feel like you can't get up and get out, God will fight on your behalf. I was broken, hurt, angry, and empty. God healed me. Even when I couldn't hold myself up, he held me in his highest regard. Our journey started, and we now live in our hallway of healing.

May God bless the readers of this testimony. I pray that your life is blessed beyond measure. In the darkest parts of your pain, there is healing. There is a calm after the storm. God heals.

Chapter 1

A NEW JOURNEY

On February 16, 2014, I married my best friend. I was seven months pregnant, and life was about to change. I had just become a wife, and almost two months later, I became a mother for the first time. On April 2, 2014, at 5:26 a.m., I gave birth to a baby boy who weighed seven pounds and ten ounces and was nineteen and a half inches long. Life had just begun for me again.

The journey of motherhood was amazing, scary, and a blessing all in one. I never believed I could love a being as much as I loved the little person staring in my eyes with unconditional love and dependency. It was a moment I could have stayed in for the rest of my life. In that moment,

I experienced motherhood. I was his mom, and he was my son. His image was that of his father's.

Our journey weeks later became even more surreal. We received orders to move out of the state I had known all of my life, Maryland, to go to a state I had only visited on vacation, Florida. There was a catch. My husband would be going to Yokosuka, Japan, for two years unaccompanied while my son and I were in Florida beginning our new journey. My last days in Severn, Maryland, were exciting and hopeful for the future.

On June 12, 2014, we left for Florida. My mother would travel with us to help with our son as we prepared for move-in day. Saying goodbye to my father was difficult, as he looked at me with happiness and hurt. I knew I would miss him. I knew my father would miss spending time with me as well. We were late-night buddies. We would stay up laughing and joking into the wee hours of the night. I was and still am a daddy's girl, but it was time for dad's little girl to leave and be with her family.

We hugged and said goodbye after a family prayer.

Jeremiah 29:11 began to play in my mind as tears ran down my face. "'For I know the plans I have for you,' declares the Lord, 'plans to prosper you and not to harm you, plans to give you hope and a future.'" At this moment I knew it wouldn't be easy, but I knew it was what I needed to do.

We drove for what seemed to be hours; we stopped three times, and eleven and a half hours later, we were in Jacksonville, Florida. Palm trees were in view, and the feeling of summer was all around. I couldn't believe that I was going to be living in Florida—and without my husband and extended family. Our home would not be ready until the next day, so we stayed with a close friend. We moved into our home on June 14, 2014, becoming first-time homeowners in a newly built neighborhood in the suburbs of Florida.

A week later it was time to say goodbye to my loving and supportive mother. She could barely look at me as we pulled up to the airport. She said, "See you later," and she kissed her grandson, hugged my husband and me, and walked away swiftly. I wept until the tissue broke apart into pieces on my face. I squeezed my husband's hand just as I did when I was preparing to bring my son into the world. I was afraid and had indeed begun to depend on my husband and his direction for our family.

Weeks passed, and it was time to say goodbye to my partner. A few days before his departure, he surprised me and flew my mother back into town to help me begin to navigate life without him temporarily. I was so excited to see her face again, and I burst into tears; he knew I needed her, and seeing her, I knew she needed me. Saying goodbye felt like it was happening all over again, and it was happening way too fast.

It was time to begin life, raising my son without the physical support of his father. I was to become protector and director. I was officially becoming the head of my household. My husband was leaving. The night before he left, it was painful looking at the one who was leaving to serve our country. My husband deployed August 16, 2014, at five in the morning and headed to Japan. At least temporarily, life would be different. I felt like I truly had to grow up and figure it out on my own. I had to make decisions without the one who usually figured it all out.

We left the house and drove toward the airport. Before we got there, my hands began to sweat as if I had washed them and forgotten to dry them. My chest was beating as if I had taken a three-mile run. My heart felt broken and torn as if I had just lost someone I loved. He got out of the truck and kissed me. And even though I appeared strong, I was a wreck inside. He leaned over into the arms of my mother and kissed our son. "I love you, son," he said. Tears fell from his face, and he walked away.

I immediately felt afraid, alone, and worried. I stood and watched him navigate his way into the airport until I was directed to move the truck. In my mind, time had frozen; there was no light at the end of the tunnel for us. I wanted him home, but I knew the job he took on to serve our country, the United States of America, was of great importance. I thought about how I would manage alone without my husband and family. I wondered who I could trust to help me navigate the area.

Months later I got acquainted with neighbors and coworkers who eventually became family. I began to navigate my way through Jacksonville, and I began to get comfortable with life apart from what had been familiar. I was truly becoming independent. God was directing me through life. Family was just a flight and a fare away. I could do this and needed to do it. I was, for the first time, becoming truly independent. It felt amazing. I was officially the bird that flew out of the nest.

Chapter 2

SURPRISE: FIRST TRIMESTER

After two long years of being alone and raising our two-year-old son, my husband was finally coming home from deployment. I was happy, nervous, and excited. I had prepared our home for his arrival. The floors shined as if I had entered a floor-mopping contest. Our bedroom had a delicate, sweet aroma that would capture his attention. My man was finally coming home. We had decided months before to try for another beautiful blessing.

One of the happiest days of my life was July 17, 2017—my husband was finally home, safe and sound. I no longer had to play both mom and dad. At last I could sleep without constantly getting up in the middle of the night to check and recheck the doors and alarm. I was grateful that a time of rest had finally arrived. My king, lover, best friend, companion, prayer partner, and protector was home.

Three weeks after my husband's arrival I began to feel sick. The hours at work began to feel like days. I was weak, emotional, tired, and drained. I equated my body changes to the overexcitement of my husband being home and possibly changes to my environment working in a childcare facility. Another week passed, and "Rose" had not arrived, so I decided to go online to order a pregnancy test. I thought, *Could I possibly be pregnant?* A big part of me said, *No way, he just got home—not this fast.* Another part of me kept saying, *Yes, you are!*

Around the second week of August, I finally decided to stop looking at the test, and I took it. Ten seconds went by as I waited for the results. After the brief wait, I walked into my bathroom and saw the word *pregnant* displayed on the screen. I was amazed, nervous, and extremely proud that I was going to experience the joys of motherhood again. I immediately ran to my husband and told him we were pregnant. He was smiling with nervousness and excitement. We told our son that he was going to be a big brother, and we laughed with joy. Our son responded to the news with the words, "Okay, Mommy." We laughed, and the journey of pregnancy began.

The first trimester was tough to bear; it was nothing like my first pregnancy with my son. Every day started with severe vomiting and extended time in the bathroom. Work was the most difficult place to be. I was always vomiting and feeling severe nausea. I thought, *How will I get through this pregnancy and work simultaneously?* As the days went by, I frequently made trips to the emergency room. I often experienced spotting and fatigue. The possibilities of losing my unborn child became a slight reality. This pregnancy began to feel more draining than exciting. We pressed on anyway, awaiting the day when we would meet the little person who kept us visiting the emergency room.

As the days passed, the feeling of sickness never seemed to lessen. I began to look up home remedies to minimize my symptoms. I tried mints, ginger ale, pregnancy drops, teas, salt, and ginger. But nothing seemed to work. I was hanging on for dear life at some points during the first trimester. The comfort of my family, coworkers, sisters, and friends made the journey worth it. I truly had a great support system.

My sisters on the job had indeed taken over the role of my protectors. I was not allowed to stand long, walk long, or even talk long. For nine hours of my working day, I was monitored. Best friends from home were constantly on standby awaiting any calls. It was unbelievable to have coworkers and friends who took on the role of family in the absence of my own. God had shown me that family is not dependent on a blood connection. It was a heart connection. To have found this regard meant more to me than life itself. I could finally call Jacksonville, Florida, "home."

After a few weeks, the sickness began to subside. I was starting to be myself again, I believed. I began to appreciate pregnancy. I embraced the forming of my belly and the expanding of my hips. I was what they call in the music world "feeling myself." The weight was going in all the proper places, and I still found a way to prance around my husband as I had done when we were dating. I was ready to face pregnancy head on. At that moment God whispered to me, "Do not be anxious about anything, but in every situation, by prayer and petition, with thanksgiving, present your requests to God. And the peace of God, which transcends all understanding, will guard your hearts and your minds in Christ Jesus" (Philippians 4:6–7). I was in complete rest and peace knowing that God was in control.

Chapter 3

HOPEFUL: SECOND TRIMESTER

We made it out of the first trimester and into the second trimester. We began to announce the excitement of our pregnancy to friends and family. We played guessing games and sent surprise video messages via text. We took a deep breath as a sign of relief that we had finally gotten out of what we called the scary zone. We were having a baby. My son was going to be a big brother. I was thrilled but nervous.

Later that week we scheduled an anatomy appointment to determine the sex of the baby. The day of surprise had finally come. We entered what I termed the "determination room." After a few moments of checking the baby's vitals, the technician revealed that the baby was a girl. I remember saying to the technician, "I don't know how to do hair. Are you sure it's a girl?" She replied, "I'm positive you guys have a girl." We were happy and felt blessed.

As we walked out of the anatomy room, two of my sisters from work greeted us. They had been listening behind the door as we were learning the sex of the baby. They seemed as if they were acting out a scene from the movie *Mission: Impossible.* They had decided to spy on us because they did not want to wait with everyone else until next Monday morning for the baby reveal celebration. I was angry and filled with laughter all at once. They had cheated, but they were baby Naomi's godmothers and my big sisters, so I got over it. Naomi was loved sincerely before her birth.

I went home and began creating the gender-reveal boxes for the baby show celebration at work on that upcoming Monday. I built two boxes, one blue and one pink. The blue box was decorated and labeled boy. The pink box was decorated and labeled girl and filled with pink streamers.

Monday arrived, and it was time to reveal the gender of the baby. It had been predetermined that my supervisors would help me announce the sex of the baby to the staff. We all walked out on the toddler playground to reveal the secret to the staff members who were available to attend. My supervisors, Captain and the Eagle as I called them, each held a box. Everyone stood still, watching and waiting to see which box would reveal the gender. On the count of three, they flipped the boxes upside down, and pink streamers and confetti flew everywhere. Captain had held the box that contained the baby's identity. The playground was filled with screams and cheers. The secret was revealed. The baby was a girl. It sounded as if I was standing in the middle of an NFL game and the winning team was rejoicing.

After weeks of telling everyone that I believed I was having another boy, knowing that I was having a girl was a joy for everyone. Baby Naomi was on the way. I was surrounded by love and a lot of coworkers wearing pink shirts to support their guesses. It was an official pink day at work. Now I was free to say "she" and "her" when I was speaking of the preparation for our child. The feeling was like no other. We had made it out of the safe zone into what I called the relaxation zone.

Life was good. I was feeling great and at the happiest point of my pregnancy. I was changing, and my husband was beginning to order and prepare her room. We decorated the room in shades of pink and white. Her room was perfect; it was made for our princess. The most important part of the second trimester was that every appointment I had was considered excellent and on target with expectations.

We entered the happy zone, the final trimester. We were discussing in more detail the life we planned to live with her. My husband and I discussed whom she would mimic, whom she was going to look like, and how she would follow her brother foot to foot. We even discussed how we would prepare her savings so she would never have to worry about getting through life financially. We made sure our hearts and minds were ready for our princess. We prepared our home to welcome her home. We finished her room on Saturday, February 4, 2017. We were ready. Nothing prepared us for what was to come next as we waited for her arrival.

Chapter 4

DEVASTATION: THIRD TRIMESTER

Sunday, February 5, 2017, changed our lives forever. At twenty-nine weeks and one day pregnant, I woke up feeling on top of the world. It was another day toward the finish line of birthing my second child, Naomi Marie Smith. We were on the final leg of the race. My husband decided to take my son and me out to lunch, and we enjoyed some southern barbecue. The sky was cold, cloudy and drizzling that day. It was just another day of living and following the routine. I had felt as great as I had ever felt except for being a little tired.

At around two in the afternoon, we headed home from

the restaurant. We arrived at our home and decided to lie down and rest for a bit. For some reason, I couldn't sleep. I realized that I had not felt the baby move all day. In fact, I had not felt movement since the night before. I began to worry. I was confused about why she hadn't moved. Naomi was an active baby. *My sweet baby hasn't moved all day*, I thought. She always was moving in the womb as if she was at a moon-bounce party. Her movement had been my early alarm clock for the past several months.

I began to try all the tricks I knew before calling the doctor. I tried eating chocolate; I moved my tummy around, drank juice, and even played loud music. Naomi just wouldn't budge. Deep down I felt like something might not be right. My intuition softly started to alarm me. Just to verify she was okay, I decided to contact the on-call nurse. After giving my symptoms, I was asked to come into the hospital to check and verify her movements and vitals.

I arrived at the hospital around four in the afternoon. I went in feeling like everything was going to be okay.

I wanted to ignore the negative little feeling I had that something was wrong. I believed it was going to be another visit where I was told not to worry and that she would be okay. I knew I was going to hear, "You can go home; the baby is doing great as usual."

I was directed to the maternity room. I was asked to give a urine sample and wait on the bed until the nurse came in to check my vitals. The nurse arrived minutes after I came out of the restroom. I lay down on the table and prepared for the nurse to apply all the monitors. She began to check my vitals, and her face went from a smile to a sudden look of shock and sadness. The nurse said, "I can't seem to get a heartbeat. I will need to get another nurse to try." Suddenly my heart dropped to the floor. I was terrified; I knew something was wrong.

Four nurses rushed into the room, and each of them tried to find her heartbeat. The last nurse turned and said, "I'm sorry; there is no heartbeat. We have declared her deceased." I screamed as if I was running for my life. In this moment my life changed forever. The nurses walked out, but one stayed while I made the hardest phone calls of my life. The first call was to my husband. He answered and said, "Hello," and while hysterically crying, I yelled, "I need you to come to the hospital. She is dead." My husband responded repeatedly, "Nooooo, please don't tell me that."

My body went into what felt like shock. I felt as if I had gone out of mind to a place of no return. How was this happening to me? I couldn't believe it. I felt like I was in a nightmare fighting to wake up. I wanted to save my baby. I wanted her to wake up. The nurse who stayed in the room began to pray with me. She then turned to me and said, "How would you like to proceed? You may go home and come back to have her removed after making a decision." I decided to have her removed immediately because I couldn't face the fact that she was inside me with no heartbeat. I wanted to go back to yesterday and save her.

Reality was staring me in the face, and I was numb. She wasn't going to arrive. Naomi was going to my memory, not my reality. I was not going to bring her home. At that moment my thoughts shifted. No longer would I be giving birth to my child; I was going to be giving birth to God's angel. I had become the one out of four mothers who give birth to a stillborn across the United States. I had become the story that I once watched on Lifetime. I was one of the reported statistics of 2017. I immediately became sick, angry, hopeless, envious, embarrassed, hurt, defeated, fearful, removed, empty, and violated. My body at that moment felt dirty and useless.

Moments later I walked to the delivery room where the staff would induce labor. Disconnected as I was at the time, I entered a cold and dimly lit room. I undressed and got into my gown, and the process began. Nurses were always coming in and out taking blood, checking vitals, and trying to keep us as comfortable as humanly possible, considering the situation. I will never forget the emptiness I felt lying on the table like a corpse. I felt like a failure. I felt like a mother who couldn't protect her child. I felt like I had failed my family.

I didn't understand why I hadn't picked up the signs

earlier. I went back and replayed how the physicians and nurses described every doctor's appointment as perfect. I was angry and trying to process mentally that I was lying on a cold bed about to deliver my stillborn child. The overwhelming part of the situation was having to give birth to a baby and hear no sound after she arrived. After hours of preparation, my water broke, and the wait began. Moments later I began to contract. The doctor came in and said, "This may take a while so try to get some rest."

I remember looking up to the ceiling as I called on God. "Please, God, don't allow this to go on for hours." As soon as I looked down, a gush of water came forth, and she began to crown. My husband and a friend alerted the nurse to come in, and the process started. I knew I would never be the same again. Hearing the words "I'm sorry" began to sound repetitive—like nails pounding into my already bleeding heart. All I could think of was that I would be leaving with empty hands. No baby. Naomi had become an angel in heaven.

Chapter 5

EMPTY HANDS

"Okay, honey, push," the doctor said. Tears began to roll down my already wet and blushed face. I pushed, and she came out after only one attempt. The room was silent. This birth was not anything like the birth of my son; when he came out, he alarmed the place with the authority of his cry. Time seemed to stop; it was silent. Naomi was there but silent. There was no sign of life in her and no sound of arrival. I was angry, confused, and heartbroken. I went through delivery to arrive at what I believed was a dark and lonely place. I cried out, "God, no, please wake her up." She continued to sleep. My reality went from expectation to a nightmare. Although all was silent, there was a feeling of peace over the room.

The most difficult thing to understand was that she was not going to come home with us. I had to accept that she was in the arms of my Lord and Savior, Jesus Christ. As empty as I felt, I knew that eventually I would grow to understand that God still had a plan for my life. Moments after her delivery, I watched my husband begin to grieve while holding and gently rocking her in his arms, admiring the beauty of her existence. She silently slept, but I knew that she was not going to wake up. Deep down I wished that she would wake up and cry. She didn't.

After several moments, I finally got the strength to hold her. I couldn't stand watching her beautiful but lifeless body. I held her and wept. I said, "Mommy loves you and will forever."

That next morning my husband and I were greeted with support and love from coworkers who had become family. They stood by us until we left the hospital. After a brutal twenty-four hours, it was time to go home. We were discharged and given permission to leave. We were not leaving with our daughter; we were leaving with her memory box. I was angry, hurt, and again devastated. As I walked to the door, I felt my body collapse onto the floor. My legs felt paralyzed; I was overwhelmed and felt lifeless. I was leaving with empty hands and a mustard seed of faith that I would be okay.

The wheelchair ride from the sixth floor to the front of the hospital felt like a lifetime. My husband had gotten the car and picked me up in front of the hospital. I was assisted into the vehicle with condolences. It was still surreal; I was going to go home without my child. I looked down at my stomach, and it was confirmation that I was no longer pregnant. I was going home and leaving her body at a hospital. I felt as if God had forgotten me. I was trying to determine what I had done to deserve the loss of my child.

Driving home, I recalled Job 1:21 and said, "Naked I came from my mother's womb, and naked I will depart. The Lord gave, and the Lord has taken away; may the name of the Lord be praised." Physically I was unable to thank the Lord at this moment, but my heart and mind would not turn from him even in my anger, hurt, and frustration. I knew I was going to need the Lord more than ever. I was crawling in pain and had to learn to walk in healing. I knew it couldn't begin to take place without him.

John 3:16 came to mind. "For God so loved the world that he gave his only begotten son that whosoever believeth in him would not parish but would have everlasting life." Even in the darkest part of my life, I knew there was a pinpoint of light shining through. God was still holding my family and me in his arms. I didn't and still don't understand, but I still believe that the righteous would not be forsaken.

Ecclesiastes 3:1–4 reads, "For everything there is a season, and a time for every matter under heaven: a time to be born, and a time to die; a time to plant, and a time to pluck up what is planted; a time to kill, and a time to heal; a time to break down, and a time to build up;

a time to weep, and a time to laugh; a time to mourn, and a time to dance." I believed at that moment that I would dance. I envisioned myself healed and given a second chance, although at the moment I was hanging on for dear life. I knew that I would not be a victim but a victor. I knew I had to take my pain and turn it around. Losing Naomi was the most painful feeling I had ever felt. I wanted to wash away the pain. I wanted to run away and start over where people never knew I was even pregnant.

Dealing with what had been normal was now a dark place. I turned and began to reach out for help to deal with and understand what my life was going to be. I knew that staying down could be tragic. I had too many people to help with my story. I had a husband who needed his wife, a son who needed his mother, and a mind that needed me. I gave myself permission to cry, scream, etc. But I also gave myself permission to get up in the name of Jesus and continue living life the way God had designed and the way Naomi would have wanted.

My relationship with Christ has not made grieving my child comfortable; it has given me hope and faith that trouble doesn't last forever. I will come to understand it better by and by as the old folk song mentioned.

Chapter 6

SUPPORT

February 6, 2017, was the beginning of my new normal. I would never think of life the same again. I would never look at pregnancy the same again. The innocence of the joy of pregnancy was temporarily erased in my mind. I held tight to the fact that God had to be near. I could give up, or I could survive. I chose to survive. Isaiah 41:10 reads, "Fear not, for I am with you; be not dismayed, for I am your God; I will strengthen you, I will help you, I will uphold you with my righteous right hand." I knew even in the deepest trenches of my pain that God was still with me.

As life moved forward, the calls began. Chaplains,

friends, family, bereavement counselors, etc. called with condolences and prayers. It was becoming more real, more painful, and it was my reality. I was the mother of a stillborn child. I didn't want to be, but it was what I was called to be. Days later I began to seek out counseling services. I had no idea where to start, what I was looking for, or what I needed. I just understood I needed help. I found a support group to attend.

I was nervous, scared, and hopeful when I arrived for the meeting at seven in the evening. As I walked in, a smiling chaplain greeted me, and I greeted her with a plastered smile and a firm shake. I sat down on a couch and waited for the arrival of others experiencing the same or similar pain. Minutes later, everyone who was going to be at the meeting arrived. It was a diverse mixture of individuals, each sharing their stories as we went around the circle. After each story, I listened to my heart begin to break, but I refused to cry. I had to be tough and wasn't going to be vulnerable in front of strangers.

Finally it was my turn, and I kept my story short. I

did not want to cry. As the meeting progressed, I learned about the journey on which I was going to embark. I also learned that no matter what I did or what meetings I attended, I could not get rid of the pain. At that moment I wanted to run, but my body, sitting on the couch, was numb and not moving. My heart was broken and hurting. My head was filled with millions of emotions that I could not put into words. The stories began to take me back to the night of her birth. Tears began to fill my eyes until they were sitting on the bottom of my eyelids. I kept telling myself not to cry.

The chaplain turned to me and said, "What are you doing to take care of yourself?" Silence filled the room. All eyes were on me as the members awaited my response. I was the center of attention. The tears that sat on the bottoms of my eyelids fell down my face. I responded, "I have been staying alone in my home after two-and-a-half-mile walks around the neighborhood every morning." I continued to talk about how empty I had been feeling and that I wanted the pain to go away. I just wanted to be normal again.

The room continued to be silent until a lady called out, "There is no normal. You will now find a new normal."

Two of the most memorable things I took away from the meeting were (1) the types of people I would encounter, and (2) that I could try—it was possible to have a child after a stillbirth. The chaplain talked about four types of individuals: First is the person who will ask the bereaved mother, "Are you still grieving?" The second type is the one who wants to overspiritualize the bereaved mother's situation. The third individual doesn't know what to say and runs the opposite way from the bereaved mother. The last type is the family and friends who stand beside the bereaved in support for the duration of her life.

I held on to this as a part of my healing. Not everyone would have the right words to say. The words that some said to me had already helped and hurt. Deep down I knew that my focus was not on the words that hurt me but on the love that God had shown me through the people

I had in my life. The chaplain advised us to continue healing, and the meeting ended. I drove home wondering if participating in a group was a good thing. I left feeling worse than I had felt going in. I began to pray, asking God to guide me and give me strength. I wanted the power Job had when everything he had known was taken away. I wanted to heal.

The drive home was long and quiet. I arrived home and fell into the doorway crying as I tried to figure out how I would get through this. I was fearful of what my life would look like post-stillbirth. I couldn't go out in public, the color pink made me sick, crying babies felt like a punch in the stomach, and the sight of pregnant women made me angry. Was I normal? Was this the way to grieve? Was there something wrong with me? I did not know where to begin.

God's word in 2 Timothy 1:7 reads, "For God has not given me a spirit of fear, but of power and love and a sound mind." It was time to rise and activate the little faith that I held onto. I didn't want to live in pain, but I didn't know how I was going to survive my baby's death. I was going to do things that I had never done before to arrive at my healing. I was going to get to my hallway of healing by leaning on God and God alone. I had also begun to work out again. It was a healthy part of my new normal. I was determined to get back to my prepregnancy weight. I also resolved to take care of myself and to get mentally healthy again.

I had started attending Bible study at my church home. It lifted me up in my darkest moments. 1 Peter 5:6–7 reads, "Humble yourselves, therefore, under God's mighty hand, that he may lift you up in due time. Cast all your anxiety on him because he cares for you." I knew at that moment that I was in the fight of my life. I needed to give it all I had. The devil was riding my back, and I was determined to throw him off. I did not want to die in my pain. I did not want to become lifeless. I would never get over the loss of my daughter, but I was intent on surviving it. I was determined that her memory would live on, that she would never be forgotten. I was going to fight to be better than I had ever been.

It had been a month since her death, and it was time for the first transition into my new normal. I had to go back to work and face everything and everyone that reminded me of all I had known and lost before and after her death. It was going to be the second most devastating part of my stillborn experience. I had been calling on the Lord, and I heard him say, "The righteous cry out, and the Lord hears them; he delivers them from all their troubles. The Lord is close to the brokenhearted and saves those who are crushed in spirit. The righteous person may have many troubles, but the Lord delivers him from them all" (Psalm 34:17–19). I was dependent on the Lord and needed him. My life was depending on it. It was time to go back to work.

Chapter 7

BACK TO WORK

On March 27, 2017, I awoke at seven o'clock to the sound of my alarm. It was officially time to return to work after the loss of Naomi. I was anxious yet hopeful that the day would be great but also realistic that it could be the hardest thing I would go through. I arose from the bed and prepared my son and me for the day. It was time to face another fear I'd had since being home after her death. The time had come to face the place where I would be surrounded by infants, pregnant women, and other things that triggered thoughts of her death. After getting prepared for work, I headed for the door. I got into my car feeling numb but ready to hit the road. The drive felt long and never-ending.

When we arrived at work, I parked, and we got out the car. My son and I began to walk toward the front door. My hands started to sweat when we were greeted outside by a friend who helped me carry my son. My legs felt weak, and my hands began to shake. I entered the building to friendly but uncomfortable faces. The words I heard as I walked down the hall were a fast *hello* or *hi*. I was uncomfortable, and I could tell everyone else was. I could imagine wearing the other shoe. Some people simply did not know what to say and wanted to avoid saying things that could upset me. Some spoke, and some didn't.

I dropped off my son at his classroom and headed toward my room. I entered to smiling faces, caramel popcorn, gifts, and tight hugs from friends. I began to recall the four types of people that the chaplain had mentioned. Surrounding me were the individuals who would truly have my back and the ones who would have nothing to say. I couldn't determine if it was the stares or the brief words from my coworkers that hurt the most. At that moment I felt like I had truly hit rock bottom. I was greeted by coworkers who were still pregnant and coworkers who did not know what to say. Parents who were genuinely shocked and concerned about my recovery also made their way over to welcome me. The most difficult greeting I faced after returning to work was from a mother who approached me, holding her six-week-old baby, and apologized for my loss as she stared at me with sadness.

My work was a constant reminder of what I didn't have and what I had lost. One of my duties was to take the kids outside to play on the playground. I was standing and watching the children play when a parent noticed me and shouted, "Where is your baby?" Tears welled up in my eyes as I replied, "She passed away in my belly." The woman looked at me in a state of shock. I realized as I was standing there and looking back that there would never be a normal.

In my mind, I was officially the woman who had lost her baby and returned to work. I was not able to enjoy the moment that other mothers experienced as they walked the halls. I was angry, sad, and humiliated that I was unable to share in the moment. Although I felt blessed to have my son, I yearned for my daughter. I wanted to hold my new baby. I wanted to feel her body move and sleep in my hands. I wanted Naomi back.

My job was feeling like a constant reminder that she was not here anymore. I questioned how I'd survive this pain nine hours a day, five days a week. In my mind I was not going to survive this; in fact, every day at work was torture. I had no voice and no choice. I knew that my journey would be rough and that I had to get through it, but I did not know how. I was overwhelmed with anger and sadness. I was counting down the moment that the clock would read five thirty and that I would be able to leave for the day. It had been only a half day, and I was struggling to get through it. Facing an entire day seemed impossible. I could only deal with today and had to leave the unknown, unknown.

By the middle of the week, work began to feel possible,

but it still felt difficult to bear. I was always seeing and greeting parents with small infants. I felt as if everyone around me had given birth to little girls, and I had no choice but to embrace them all with a smile because it was my job. The other side of me wanted to run out immediately. By Thursday I began to feel stronger. I started to feel that although I had to be there now, it would be temporary. I believed that God had better for me; I just needed to hold on.

I needed to find a reason to smile even if it was the hope of my future. I could not stay in this depressed state forever. I just had to stay busy, move fast, and try to avoid situations where Naomi would be the focus of the conversation. The hugs helped but hurt.

Friday finally arrived, and I had made it through the week. I was officially proud of myself. This was the first week but also the first mountain I had climbed publicly. My healing in that time was not just my own but others' as well. My strength began to encourage others, who could only imagine how I felt and needed to see my improvement.

I started to feel like my pain would leave sooner than later and would eventually turn into power. I would not let her death overwhelm me. I wanted her memory to remind me that I was blessed, still am blessed, and would continue to be blessed.

There are not always explanations in life for why things happen; all I know is that I could not get through them without the help of my Lord and Savior, Jesus Christ. I could feel the prayers of those who were genuinely concerned about my mental and emotional well-being.

Work started to feel like more than just a job and a place of sadness; it felt like a place where I could truly say I was loved and cared for. It was a place where I knew I had to be strong and still inspire and encourage individuals who needed my smile, laughter, and joking personality. I was learning that I could hold my head high and begin to see the brighter side of every day. I also knew that it was time for me to grow and move forward. The environment was not the best for my mental health anymore. Constantly viewing and caring for small babies was too much to bear. I knew it was time to start the process of leaving, so I began to set my mind to even greater possibilities. It was time to go and grow.

Chapter 8

HALLWAY TO HEALING

Over the two months following Naomi's death, I had learned that God makes no mistakes. I had even begun to understand that my plans were not my own. I remained confident. Life was not over, and I could try again. I learned that sharing my experience with the world had not made and would not make me weak. I had learned that my life was not over. I also realized that no matter how close to God I was, it never would take the pain away, but it would comfort me through it.

If I could share anything with anyone in my situation or a similar situation, I would say don't give up. I would say allow yourself to feel every emotion. Allow yourself to feel every pain. Allow yourself to be helped by those in your corner. Surround yourself with positivity. Be okay with cutting off anything that does not permit you to grow. Fall, but get back up.

I was determined to get back up. I cried, but I wiped away my tears. I was on a pathway of self-destruction, but I found a reason to live. God needed me to share my story, and I needed to save someone going through a traumatic experience. I had to grab hold of God, family, and the support of friends. I had to realize there would still be bumps in the road and more tears to cry, but I knew that the Lord would never leave or forsake me. I had to grab hold of that mustard seed of faith.

Matthew 17:20 reads, "He replied, 'Because you have so little faith. Truly I tell you, if you have faith as small as a mustard seed, you can say to this mountain, "Move from here to there," and it will move. Nothing will be impossible for you.'" Nothing is impossible although it may feel impossible. I wouldn't allow the pain of my baby's loss to overtake the joy of her memory. My daughter, Naomi, brought a joy in my life that I will never forget. I learned from her the real joy of motherhood. I learned to love with even more passion. I learned not to take life so seriously. I learned to love my husband in a new way.

My husband and I began to grow closer than we had ever been. I needed his comfort, and he needed mine. Although we grieved differently, our understanding of the love Naomi left for us would never die. I loved my son with more integrity, more compassion, and more patience. I learned to draw nearer to Christ. I found out in my reality that tomorrow is not promised. Live each day the best way you know how.

I will never completely be okay with her loss, but I have found ways to walk through this journey of life understanding that God makes no mistakes. God is the God of a second chance. We will try again and not fear. Knowing why things happen is not necessary; his will is. Giving up was the easiest thing I could do. Going on and becoming better is what I needed to do. The will of God is not for us to understand, but we must follow it.

I would have never dreamed that I could find healing in this situation. I could never have imagined finishing this book while going through bereavement. I found it in myself to ask God for courage, peace, and strength to get through this piece of inspiration. God softly whispered to me, "I can do all things through Christ who strengthens me" (Philippians 4:13). I had become a soldier in the army of the Lord. I had gone through one of the toughest battles of my life. I had survived.

I was not a victim; I was a victor. I was not a statistic; I was a story. I was not going to die; I would live. I was not just a mom of a stillborn; I was the mother of an angel. I was and would become everything the Lord had designed for me to be. I could finally rehearse Psalm 23 out loud while going through this new normal: "The Lord is my shepherd I shall not want. He maketh me to lie down in green pastures: he leadeth me besides the still waters. He restoreth my soul: he leadeth me in the paths of righteousness for his name's sake. Yea though I walk through the valleys of the shadow of death, I will fear no evil for thou are with me; thy rod and thy staff they comfort me. Thou preparest a table before me in the presence of mine enemies: thou anointest my head with oil; my cup runneth over. Surely goodness and mercy shall follow me all the days of my life: and I will dwell in the house of the Lord forever." Amen.

The journey is not over; the hallway to healing has just begun. I will continue to live on, and Naomi's legacy will never be forgotten for she brought my family back to Christ. Naomi was on borrowed time and always had belonged to the Lord. I will never know what she would have been like, but I believe she came and completed her assignment. She served a purpose and now is sitting with God—my angel, my princess, my peace. Naomi will live in our hearts for the rest of our lives. Thank you, Lord.

Seven Days Stronger

MONDAY: HEALING

I am one step closer to my healing. I am a survivor.
I carried, I conquered, I made it through, and I'm
still alive. I am a mirror of faith. A beautiful being.
An example of strength. God has me in his hands.

Scripture:

Psalm 30:2 (NIV)

Lord my God, I called to you for

help, and you healed me.

Tuesday: Courage

I am one step closer to my destiny. Courage is what I need. I am filled with the hope of today. I will go on, knowing that my life is not over. In fact, I am just beginning. I will conquer every fear with my courage. God is my strength.

Scripture:

1 Corinthians 16:13 (NIV)

Be on guard; stand firm in the faith;

be courageous; be strong.

WEDNESDAY: LOVE

While the world trusts man, I choose to trust God. I will love in my loss. I will be patient with my healing. I will trust God in my pain. I have hope because I know God loves me. I am his most prized possession. God sees me.

Scripture:

1 Peter 5:6–7 (NIV)

Humble yourselves, therefore, under the mighty hand of God so that at the proper time he may exalt you, casting all your anxieties on him, because he cares for you.

Thursday: Peace

Peace lives in me. I will overcome every obstacle
placed in my way because I am needed. I am
a child of God. His power strengthens me.
His love keeps me. God is in control.

Scripture:

Philippians 4:7 (NIV)
And the peace of God, which transcends
all understanding, will guard your
hearts and minds in Christ Jesus.

Friday: Faith

I will have joy. I will exercise my faith. I will
finish the work God has given me. I will lean
on him for direction. I will trust in him. There
are no mistakes. God has a plan for my life.

Scripture:

Jeremiah 29:11 (NIV)

"For I know the plans that I have for you," declares
the Lord, "plans to prosper you and not harm
you, plans to give you a hope and a future."

Saturday: Joy

Joy will overtake my life. I will regain everything I have lost. I will have a fresh start to a planned life. God has given me the tools I need to be successful. The goodness of the Lord surrounds me. God will restore my joy.

Scripture:

1 Thessalonians 5:16–18 (NIV)

Rejoice always, pray continually, give thanks in all circumstances; for this is God's will for you in Christ Jesus.

Sunday: Hope

I will hope for tomorrow because Jesus lives. He
has given me salvation. I am free. I choose to live,
love, and laugh. God is with me. He is healing,
He is peace, He is hope, He is courage, He is love,
He is joy, and He is faith. God is my Savior.

Scripture:

Romans 15:13 (NIV)

May the God of hope fill you with all joy and
peace as you trust in him, so that you may overflow
with hope by the power of the Holy Spirit.

Acknowledgments

Tomorrow is not promised in my journey of love and loss. I have particular people in my life who have helped me on my journey of healing and to whom I need to give a rose. I never imagined I would have to go through such a tragic loss. I also never imagined that I would have so many people show me such unconditional love.

I would like to give my first rose to my husband, "Smitty." Thank you for being my rock, my sidekick. Thank you for putting yourself to the side at times to help me mourn and deal with our loss. You not only have protected my heart but you also have protected our love during this difficult time. Thank you for stepping up and becoming Mom and Dad at home so that I could heal. I love you.

I would like to give my next roses to my mother, Janice; my father, Wayne; my brother, Wayne; and my sister, Charmaine. Thank you all for taking the time to wipe my tears, hold my hand, walk with me, and pray for and with me during our loss. There is no problem that we have ever faced that we did not get through together.

My next roses go to my best friends, Andrea and Amanda. Thank you for staying loyal and loving for the past twenty years. I am making it through this journey with your constant smiles and thoughts and your continued prayers.

The next rose goes to Felicia. You were the first person I met when I moved to Florida. Not only did you help me navigate Florida, but you also helped me get through mothering a small child along the way. Thank you for being who you are. You have truly blessed my family.

Roses also go to my sister-friends Carline, Keesha, Gwen, Angie, Michelle, Brenda, and Lisa. Thank you for being a rock to my husband, our son, and me through our loss. We have bonded over the years and become family. Thank you, ladies, for the constant prayers, help, and love that you have given my entire family. Thank you for taking turns caring for our son when it got tough. Thank you for the prayers and patience. I sincerely love you beautiful ladies.

Last but not least I would like to thank my NAS JAX CDC family, friends, and extended family for your prayers and words of encouragement. It has blessed our family more than you will ever know.

Naomi

Your life was not long lived, but your memory will carry on forever. You came in this world to remind us that tomorrow is not promised, but God's word is. You have taught me to continue to be strong and hold my head up high. You have taught me that I can accomplish anything I set my mind to accomplish. You taught me to be strong in my darkest hour. Naomi, you were the very image of an angel. I vow to keep your memory alive with continued love, laughter, and faith. I promise never to stop believing in my God-given calling in life. My first book is dedicated to you. *Twenty-Nine Weeks and One Day* has completely changed my life for the better. I will forever and always adore the child that you were. I was blessed to have carried and loved you. You are now with God, and I will live my days out making you proud.

Love always,

Mommy

Printed in the United States
By Bookmasters